The Beast

Story by Chris Bell

Illustrations by Luke Jurevicius

Rigby PM Plus Chapter Books
part of the Rigby PM Program
Ruby Level

U.S. edition © 2003 Rigby Education
A division of Reed Elsevier Inc.
1000 Hart Road
Barrington, IL 60010 - 2627
www.rigby.com

Text © 2003 Thomson Learning Australia
Illustrations © 2003 Thomson Learning Australia
Originally published in Australia by Thomson Learning Australia

10 9 8 7 6 5 4 3 2 1
07 06 05 04 03

The Beast
    ISBN 0 75786 886 X

Printed in China by Midas Printing (Asia) Ltd

Contents

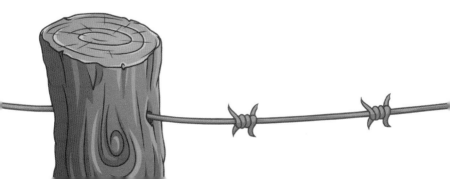

Chapter 1

As If!

Bryn stood outside the barn listening for a while. He cringed when he heard the beast snorting inside.

Was it still in its stall? Or had it broken free? There was only one way to find out. Bryn took a deep breath and threw open the barn door.

"Phew!" he sighed with relief. Drago was still inside his stall. "Come on, you lazy bull," said Bryn. "You're going back to the paddock." The enormous animal turned his head and stared at Bryn. Then he snorted again and turned back to munch from the hay trough.

"Don't ignore me, Drago. You've only lived in luxury while the paddock fence was being replaced. You're going back to where you belong – outside! Behave yourself this time."

Bryn hung back warily. He didn't trust the old bull one bit. His foot still ached from the huge bruise he'd gotten from their last meeting. That time Drago had refused to leave his paddock, and he'd stepped on Bryn's foot in protest.

Bryn didn't understand why *he* had to take Drago back to his paddock. Why couldn't Cara do it?

His stepsister was great with animals. They liked her and would do anything she wanted. But Bryn had no luck! Every time he went near an animal he came away with another bite, scratch, or bruise.

It wasn't his choice to live on a farm. Just because his family was animal crazy, it didn't mean he had to be, too.

Bryn reached over the stall and attached the lead to the metal ring through the bull's nose. Enormous eyes turned to stare at Bryn and he saw the animal tense his muscles. Bryn knew he was in for a battle.

After five minutes of tugging and pulling, begging and threatening, Bryn had failed to make the stubborn animal move at all. Drago kept munching on hay and ignored the frustrated boy beside him.

"Hey! Haven't you moved Drago back to the paddock yet?" asked Cara, coming into the barn. "Come on, old boy," she said, slapping the bull lightly on his rump.

Bryn could hardly believe his eyes. Drago backed out of the stall as if to say, "ready when you are." Bryn scowled and tugged on the rope. "Be nice to him," said Cara. "He's sweet as a lamb if you treat him right. You two could become friends!"

"Yeah right," said Bryn, dodging Drago's hooves. "He's about as sweet as a Tyrannosaurus Rex," he hissed. "And I know which one I'd rather be friends with."

As soon as they were out of Cara's sight, Drago took off at a trot, dragging Bryn along behind him.

"Slow down," Bryn yelled, struggling to keep up. But Drago trotted on even faster. Bryn dug his heels into the soft earth, but Drago kept going, pulling Bryn headfirst into the mud. Bryn dropped the lead rope. The bull looked back over his shoulder, snorted, and walked away to munch on some grass.

All the way back to the paddock the bull was well behaved, but Bryn wasn't fooled. As if he would ever be friends with that beast!

Chapter 2

Farm Life

Bryn hadn't always had a problem with animals. In fact, up until six months ago, he'd hardly had anything to do with any animal larger than their cat.

Then suddenly his parents had made their "surprise announcement" – they were all moving to a farm. "Then we can have lots of animals," they said.

Great, thought Bryn. He wasn't impressed.

Sometimes he felt Mom, Cara, and his stepfather, Rob, should have moved without him. They loved farm life and Bryn definitely did not.

He hadn't minded changing schools. And the old farmhouse, which was now their new house, was sort of fun with all its interesting rooms.

But the animals... he would never get used to them.

Rob took to farming right away. He would have happily worked around the paddocks all day, except he still had to go back to the city for office work.

Mom had immediately populated the farm with animals, but not just ordinary farm animals. She brought in extraordinary animals. At first there were only the chickens, horses, and cows, but then a truckload of llamas arrived, followed by two ostriches, and a family of deer! Then there was Drago.

The farmer who'd sold them the property insisted they keep the old bull. He'd proudly shown off Drago's blue ribbons for *Best Bull* at the local show. "Best sire in the district he is. But I can't take him with me," insisted the farmer.

So they'd inherited the stubborn, smelly, and downright mean, manure machine. Bryn despised him, yet everyone else blindly called him sweet.

Well, decided Bryn, brushing off his muddy clothes, this would be the last time the beast got the better of him. It was time to get even.

13

Chapter 3

Hot Stuff

Later that afternoon as Bryn shoveled Drago's manure into bags, his resentment toward the old bull grew inside him. He thought about his bruised foot, the bull's tug-of-war, and the final insult – shoveling manure.

He was so busy plotting his revenge that he didn't notice where he was stepping. His foot slipped from under him, and he landed on his backside in a pile of manure. Typical, thought Bryn. He finished the job resenting Drago more and more with every shovel-full.

By the time he reached the house his face glowed red with anger. He stomped around his room and couldn't concentrate on his homework. He charged out the back door yelling, "I'm going for a walk."

Before he knew it, he was passing Drago's paddock. The old bull, eating grass along the fence, looked up as Bryn passed.

"What are you looking at?" he shouted. "You manure machine!" As his temper boiled up inside him, Bryn remembered the plastic bag inside his pocket. He pulled out a handful of hot peppermints.

"Here bull, you want something to eat? Try these." He thrust his open hand through the fence. Drago moved closer.

"Go on. Take them. I dare you!" shouted Bryn. The bull nosed closer then stuck out his rough tongue and licked the peppermints right off Bryn's hand.

"Hah, got you!" shouted Bryn and he waited for the bull's reaction. But Drago chomped away on the hot peppermints like they were just a handful of sugar cubes. Blast! thought Bryn. Furiously he jumped over the fence and ran at the bull yelling, "Go away, you stupid beast. Go on. Go."

At first Drago trotted off only a few paces, but Bryn kept yelling and he began to chase the reluctant bull across the paddock. Then he waved his cap and his arms at Drago. "Get out of here, you lazy animal."

Bryn gave up and turned his back before walking back down the paddock, muttering under his breath.

Behind him Drago started snorting and began to paw the ground.

Suddenly, Bryn felt the ground begin to shudder like a small earthquake, rumbling under his feet. His heart began to thump and he glanced back over his shoulder to see Drago thundering toward him.

Bryn began to run, but the bull was gaining on him. He tripped on a clod of dirt, somersaulted, and hit the ground hard. A ton of prime beef was bearing down on him, and the pounding roared in his ears. Bryn threw his hands over his head and shut his eyes.

Bryn froze like an ice statue. The bull stopped just inches from his head. He heard Drago snort and pant over him, blowing a mix of grass and hot minty breath down his neck. The bull paced up and down, stopping every few seconds to snort over him.

Then Bryn felt Drago nuzzle down his side and start to chew at his shorts. The mints! The beast was after the mints.

Bryn thought fast. He rolled sideways, leaped to his feet, grabbed the bag of mints from his pocket, and hurled it at the bull, sending mints flying everywhere.

"Have them then," he yelled and he raced across the rest of the paddock and threw himself over the barbed wire fence, feeling the barbs scratch across the back of his leg.

He didn't even feel the pain until he put some distance between himself and Drago.

No, they would never be friends.

Chapter 4

Where's Drago?

"**I**'m not going near that bull again," announced Bryn, after he told his parents and Cara how Drago had charged at him. "And don't try to make me."

Nobody argued and Bryn was satisfied that was the end of his problem. From then on, he avoided the bull. But every time he walked past the paddock Drago would trot up to the fence and follow him along the path. "He really seems to like you now," Cara called. "Come and pat him. He wants to be your friend."

As time went by, Bryn became used to Drago following him along the fence like a confused puppy. Sometimes, feeling guilty, he would throw a couple of mints over to him. "Here, have them," he'd say, before marching on ignoring the bull's snorts. "No, that's all for today. Don't tell anyone I gave them to you."

One Saturday, Bryn walked past Drago's paddock and suddenly noticed the bull wasn't following him.

Bryn had survived an entire week without an injury or another animal accident. He was busy congratulating himself when he walked back past Drago's paddock. It did seem strange that the bull hadn't come nosing around today. Ungrateful beast, Bryn thought. He'd even bought a new bag of peppermints. Though they weren't for Drago, he quickly reminded himself.

Come to think of it, he hadn't seen the bull yesterday or the day before either. He'd gone to basketball right after school on Thursday, and he'd stayed over at Kyle's house yesterday. Where was Drago?

Bryn scanned the large paddock, but it was impossible to see all the paddock's boundaries. There was no sign of the bull under the trees.

Maybe he'd gone down to the dam for a drink? Since it was such a hot day, he was probably cooling off in the water. But there was no way Bryn cared enough about Drago to go into the paddock to check.

No way!

The next morning Bryn jogged along the path to feed the goat, and when he ran back past Drago's paddock, there was still no sign of the bull.

"Where are you, you stupid bull?" he called. Bryn sighed and bit his lip. Mom and Cara would be really worried if they found out Drago was missing. He'd better have a quick look.

"Drago!" he shouted, as he ducked between the fence wires and stepped warily into the paddock. "Drago!" But the bull didn't appear.

Bryn crept along the fence line never venturing too far from his escape route. He peered toward the distant trees in case the bull was resting in the shade.

No Drago.

The sun disappeared behind a cloud and despite the hot morning, Bryn felt a cold shiver.

Chapter 6

Hurry!

In the stillness, Bryn heard a weak bellow coming from beyond the dam wall. Before he even realized it, he was running toward the sound.

"Drago, where are you?"

He scrambled up the grassy wall, and as he came over the top his heart thumped in his chest.

Drago bellowed again from the middle of the dam. He was struggling to move. Under the water, he was firmly stuck in thick mud.

"Oh no! What have you done, you stupid bull?" yelled Bryn. "Come out here, right now." But Drago stayed where he was, bellowing pitifully.

Without a second thought, Bryn plunged into the water, mud sucking at his ankles. He tried pushing and pulling Drago, but he couldn't move the exhausted bull at all.

Drago began to slump forward onto one front knee and Bryn screamed, "No. Don't you dare give up!"

He trudged around in front of the bull and pulled the mints from the pocket of his muddy shorts. "Here, you want these, don't you? Don't you?" And he held out the mints.

He forced the bull's head up and Drago rose slowly back onto all fours. His rough tongue rasped like sandpaper across Bryn's hand. The boy looked into Drago's fading, scared eyes.

"Stay here. I'll be back with help," he yelled, and then he stumbled through the mud and up the embankment.

He flew down the paddock yelling for help. By the time he reached the yard, Mom, Rob, and Cara were running toward him.

Bryn grabbed some ropes and Drago's lead. Rob leaped onto the tractor, and they all raced to the paddock. After he opened the gate, Bryn ran up the dam wall and down the embankment. His stomach lurched as he saw Drago slumped over with his head barely above the waterline.

Drago had weakened even in the short time since Bryn had left and the poor animal didn't look as if he could hang on much longer. He splashed into the water and forced Drago's head up higher.

At that moment the tractor chugged up the dam wall. Bryn nearly cried with relief when he saw it roll over the top. "Hurry!" he screamed.

Mom and Rob tied the ropes around Drago and Bryn clipped on his lead, gently pleading with the bull to move. Tears streamed down his face leaving muddy streaks.

It seemed like hours before Rob started the tractor. It began to slowly back up the dam wall. Inch by slow inch, Drago was hauled through the mud, bellowing in protest.

31

With one final heave, the bull was free from the mud. Drago lumbered wearily up the embankment and promptly shook himself, splattering mud all over Bryn.

"You ungrateful, beast!" Bryn spluttered through a mouthful of mud. But under the mud, he was grinning broadly. Drago came over to the muddy figure and nudged him.

"Okay, I know what you want," said Bryn, laughing. "But this still doesn't mean we're friends!"